What is a Republic?

The Concise Definition You were Never Taught

John Chambers

www.ItsYourConstitution.com

ISBN-10: 1984163647
ISBN-13: 978-1984163646

This book is dedicated to you
who keep the dream of freedom alive.

Every republic has a constitution. Some constitutions are written, some are not. Some are followed, some are not. Some are cleverly put together, others are ham-handed.

The constitution of a Republic describes the elements and mechanisms that "constitute" the government. It tells the limitations of the government.

Every constitution is a mixture of basic building blocks.

The building blocks are the natural forms of government known to the ancient Greeks. They were refined by Polybius about 2200 years ago.

Below is the concise definition of Republic you were never taught. But to understand it, we have to first look at the basic building blocks, the Basic forms of Government.

If a form of government is basic or natural, it will apply not only to large social groups like Ancient Rome or the United States of America, but it would also apply to everyday societies. It would apply to a family, or a football team, for instance.

After the Basic Forms are defined, then will come the definition of Republic.

After that definition will be a brief look at the history of the concept of, and the word, "republic."

Contents

Basic Forms of Government

Aristocracy …

Monarchy …

Democracy …

Aristocracy ... the form of government that most of us first become aware of.

Most families are aristocracies. The dictionary definition is "government by the citizens deemed to be best qualified to lead." Parents, for one. The best can be those with the most education, the elders of the tribe, the most money, or the best hunters. The best are always a minority. The minority of the "best" will take care of the others (the majority) who are less able.

The advantage is that everyone is cared for. The disadvantage is that those in power could come to care only for themselves. To maintain an aristocracy, those who would be in power must disable everyone else. From the Greek *aristo-*, the best; and *-cracy*, strength or power.

It is Rule by a Minority.

Look at the groups around you ... perhaps your neighborhood Garden Club, your family, or the PTA.

Do any of those groups have only a few people who seem to run the group? Which ones?

Why do you suppose that minority is in charge?

Monarchy … rule by one person.

The essence of monarchy is "one ruler" whether a football coach, a king or a ship captain. It works well in a society with a clear purpose, such as a sports team — everyone wants to beat the team from the other town. Winning a war is best done by a single leader, directing everyone in a single plan to defeat the enemy.

The disadvantage is that the monarch could come to direct actions only for his own advantage rather than the purpose of the group. The man who would be king must find a common purpose for everyone to get behind. The defeat of an enemy is an easy target. The word comes from the Greek *mono-*, only or single; and -*archy*, ruler.

It is rule by a single person.

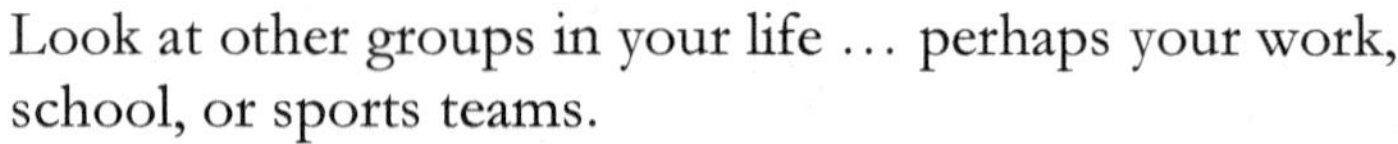

Look at other groups in your life … perhaps your work, school, or sports teams.

Do any of those groups have only one who tells others what needs to be done? Which groups?

Why do you suppose that one person is in charge?

Democracy … "government by the people" also called "majority rule."

A democracy will work when each person is able to take care of himself and also right any wrong he does to others. Such a person's voice should be heard. To have every voice heard was the hope of Pericles, the General and Statesman who started the Golden Age of Greece. It has been the defining ideal of Western Civilization ever since.

The disadvantage is that very few are able enough to right every wrong and the majority is always average. Democracy too often means mediocrity. Those who want a working democracy will make those around them more able. From the Greek *demo-*, people; and -*cracy*, strength or power.

It is rule by the many.

Look at the groups around you … perhaps your friends after school or work, a volunteer group, or a safe-neighborhood group.

Do any of those groups want to make sure everyone has a say in the decisions? Which groups?

What would happen if one or two people tried to tell everyone else what to do?

What is a Republic?

As natural as rain, a group of people will choose to be governed by a Monarchy, an Aristocracy, or a Democracy.

If most of the people in a group cannot take care of themselves,

then those who can take care of them will, and an Aristocracy will arise whether anyone wants it or not.

Similarly, if everyone in the group is headed in the same direction, a monarchy will naturally arise. The group can't help it. The people will choose someone to lead them.

Finally, if everyone in a group can take care of himself and also watch out for the well-being of others, they will form a democracy. It will arise without anyone suggesting it. It just happens.

The problem with each of the natural forms of government is that people run it. People can change from day to day. Any whim of the king, or the bureaucrats, or the mob, can take everything away from you. We need something more stable, something to count on, no matter how often the rulers change.

About 2500 years ago, the Roman Monarchy faced this very problem. The monarch had been selected by tribes that had joined together rather than destroy each other. The monarchy was a government of the tribes – a thing of the tribes.

Romans demanded a new government based on Law rather than the whim of the ruler. They formed a new government based on the People rather than the Tribes. They called their new government Res Publica, the People's Thing – what we call republic today.

The new government had elements of Monarchy in it. When a single ruler was needed, it would be there. It also had aristocratic and democratic "branches" when those are needed. Because it is made up of other forms, it is called a "mixed" government. A Republic is a Mixed government.

The genius of a mixed government is to construct it in such a way that no branch can do its job without the other branches also doing theirs. That way, no branch becomes so powerful that a whim of a ruler gains too much power. Each branch has to work with the others but, at the same time, not be ruled by any other.

A Republic is not natural. It is constructed; it is man-made. The constant struggle in a Republic is to not decay into one of the Natural forms.

The People's Thing, to serve the people, requires constant attention from the people.

Heed the famous words of Benjamin Franklin. Directly after the Constitutional Convention, the story goes, Mrs. Elizabeth Powel anxiously asked Franklin: "Well Doctor, what have we got, a republic or a monarchy?"

"A republic," answered Franklin, "if you can keep it."

End of Definition of Republic

What are the three *natural* forms of government?

How is it that a *Mixed* Government is not natural?

What can happen to a mixed government?

What do you suppose a person might do to "keep" the republic?

In as few words as possible, define the word *republic*

A Brief History of "Republic"

Plato's *Republic* is probably the first work ever written on forms of government and Constitutions.

One would think that from it, one would get a pretty good definition of a "Republic."

Not so.

The name Plato gave the work was *not* "republic" but "politeia" (pole-eye-tay-ya) which can be translated as "the relation between citizen and state" or *The Ideal State*.

Funny that later readers took the "ideal state" to be a republic.

Much of Plato's book explores "what is justice?" in a search for the best government. Certainly, justice is an excellent measure to determine if you have an *Ideal State* or not.

Plato then goes on to assert that the best rulers will be philosophers, philosopher-kings. They, in searching for the good and true, will be able to dispense justice. That means his ideal state – this is very important – is run by an elite minority. That is, the minority deemed best to rule.

That is an *Aristocracy* and he calls it so. It is not a "republic." It is an aristocracy. Of course, Plato, a philosopher, would think the philosophers should rule. We could do worse.

And his book is about to take us on that journey.

In Book 8, Plato lays out what he sees as the other four forms of government, each a corruption of the ideal.

The Aristocracy becomes corrupted into a "timocracy", an aristocracy lead not for the philosophical good and true, but for the honorable. Striving for honor, according to Plato, is not as good as the philosophical good and true.

The honorable eventually become corrupt and they aim for wealth. An "Oligarchy" ensues.

The oligarchs lend to the poor who become oppressed and revolt, ushering in a "Democracy." Plato at this point reads pretty much like Karl Marx.

The democracy cannot sustain itself because, in the same way an oligarch is greedy for money, the democratic person is greedy for freedom.

Liberty becomes libertine. Unbridled freedom leads to chaos. No one or their property is safe. The people demand something be done about it. Thus comes about the final form of government, Tyranny.

Philosopher Aristocracy decays to Honor-ocracy decays to Wealth-ocracy decays to, you guessed it, Democracy which in its turn decays to Tyranny.

Nowhere does he describe a Republic.

That was Plato. Aristotle, his student, was a more thorough observer and came up with more advanced scheme than the so-called *Republic* of Plato.

Aristotle Takes Another Look

Aristotle was Plato's prize student. I mean, literally, Aristotle as a young man sat at the feet of an elder Plato. Plato's *ideal* government was based on a philosopher's hope of the way things should be. It served as a preamble for Aristotle's new way of looking at the world.

Aristotle, rather than thinking about how thing *should* be, tried to observe things as they *actually are*.

Aristotle did not find an aristocracy of philosopher kings. He did see Oligarchies and Tyrannies and other forms. His book "Politika" means "things concerning the 'polis' (city or community)". We call it the *Politics*.

In Book 4 of the *Politics*, Aristotle observes that any government, that is to say, those who make and enforce the rules, either do it to benefit

1) the Common Good or
2) for their own selfish interest.

Further, those who make the rules are either

a) A single Person,
b) A minority of the people, or
c) the many ...

Six Forms of Government ...

Our interest is in what Aristotle called the "so-called polity or constitutional government" (upper-right corner in diagram). It is pretty much what we would call a "republic" today.

FOR THE BENEFIT OF	Single Ruler	A Minority	Rule by Many
The Common Good	Monarchy	Aristocracy	Constitutional Polity
Selfish Interest	Tyranny	Oligarchy	Democracy

Polity has a number of meanings but the one that applies is "an organized society". It has a number of parts. It is a mix-and-match of a single ruler, different minorities or "interests", even large "minorities." Its "constitution" describes the parts and how they fit together.

Some constitutional polities, Aristotle noted, tend toward aristocracy, some toward democracy, and so on. Every one of them has a "constitution" describing how the pieces fit together.

Polybius and *Res Publica*

About 100 year after Aristotle died, Polybius was born in Megalopolis, Greece to a prominent family of the city and of the Achaean League, of which Megalopolis was a member.

At the age of 33, Polybius was taken hostage by Rome in their conquest of

the League. He spent 17 years in Rome. Because of his education, he was allowed into the most important Roman homes.

He was in the perfect position to study and write on the Roman *Res Publica* as well as other histories and subjects of government. His *Histories* influenced not only the Roman historians of his time, but pretty much every historian up to and including the framers of the American Constitution.

His observations allowed him to refine Aristotle's six forms of government, and add a seventh.

First, As Aristotle observed, the three natural forms of government: Monarchy – Rule by One, Aristocracy – Rule by a Minority, Democracy – Rule by the Majority.

Each has its evil twin brother too. The seventh is a Mixed government, guided by a constitution.

FOR THE BENEFIT OF

	Single Ruler	A Minority	Rule by Many	Mixed
The Common Good	 Monarchy	 Aristocracy	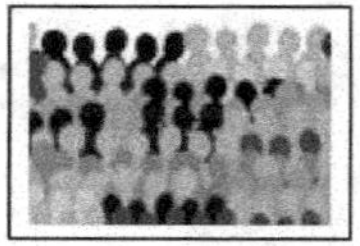 Democracy	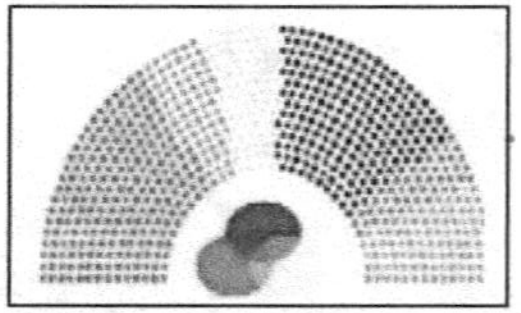 Res Publica
Selfish Interest	 Tyranny	 Oligarchy	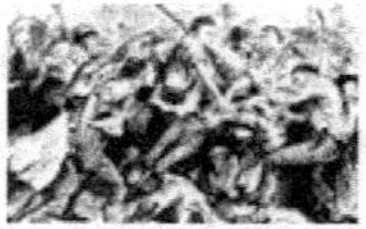 Mob Rule	

Polybius's mixed government was the beginning of "separation of powers," a vital requirement of any republic. Each "branch" of the government (a popular assembly or an elected Consul or Magistrate) has a role to fulfill.

They have to be somewhat independent of each other and yet rely upon each other to get their jobs done.

Some 1800 years after Polybius, Montesquieu picked up on the separation of powers.

Montesquieu and *République*

Baron Montesquieu (1689-1755), French aristocrat, political theorist and studied by the Founding Fathers, passed along "separation of powers."

During his time, directly before the American Revolution, the word "republic" took on a number of meanings. Its original meaning of a mixed government became muddled with ideas that would lead to the French Revolution and the Reign of Terror.

Republic and *republican* came to informally mean anyone opposed to a monarchy. Or a rabble-rouser. Or any government not a monarchy (Johnson 1755) or any government in which the people elect representatives (Webster 1828).

John Adams noted that many writers took the word to mean a representative democracy.

These definitions slosh back and forth to the point that today, a person on the street, if pressed to explain "republic" will come up with something like "it comes from *re-*, meaning 'again, like represent' and *public* meaning 'the People,' so … I guess *republic* means a government where the people are represented."

It is a valiant guess but folks are not to blame. They have never been taught.

If a government is constituted solely of representatives of the people, that government is a "representative democracy" not a *mixed* government as Aristotle and Polybius described.

Current dictionary-definitions focus on people electing representatives. One says that "the terms republic and democracy are virtually interchangeable."

A sitting U.S. Senator told me, to my face, that a republic is 'a type of democracy.'

Republic comes from *res publica*, a constitutional polity, a mixed government. It has a democratic part to it, but it is much more.

A definition of republic is necessary to understanding, in particular, the Constitution of the United States of America.

As long as this basic definition is muddled with 'democracy' or any other form of government …

As long as *Republic* is not seen as its own thing …

… the People will never restore the *People's Thing*.